66

ROMANESQUE CATALAN ART

PANEL PAINTING

THE LITTLE LIBRARY
OF ART

FIRST PUBLISHED IN 1965

TRANSLATED BY BETTINA WADIA

ACHEVÉ D'IMPRIMER
EN JANVIER 1965 PAR J. MONNIER
CLICHÉS DE CLICHÉS UNION

ROMANESQUE CATALAN ART

PANEL PAINTING

BY

JUAN AINAUD DE LASARTE

CHIEF DIRECTOR OF MUSEUMS AT BARCELONA

METHUEN AND CO LTD
11 NEW FETTER LANE, LONDON EC4

The extraordinary collection of romanesque panel painting that still survives in Catalonia is the richest to be found anywhere outside Italy.

Although religious and secular panel painting was extensive and varied, most of the examples we know formed part of the decorations of altars and sanctuaries in churches. Of these, the altar frontals are the most important. They generally depicted Christ in majesty or the Virgin, in the centre, in a type of composition that is also found in the mural paintings of apses. In later periods, their place was occupied by the seated figure of the saint to whom the church or altar was dedicated. The scenes on either side of the central figure may or may not continue the same subject depicted in those adjacent to them, but they are generally arranged in two, superposed registers. The altar frontals were often flanked by panels, which covered the sides of the altar and in which the decoration and iconography varied considerably. Sometimes, behind the altar table, a low frame was placed, containing a statuette or just a painted figure, with other figures or paintings on either side. This was the origin of the retable.

A desire to protect the altar, or to complete the decoration of the apse led to the addition of other elements later on. This was the origin of the baldequin with four columns connected by arches and surmounted by a pyramidal roof, which spread almost everywhere. In Catalonia, however, a particular model seemed to have been preferred, consisting of a large, square panel resting on two beams, one in front, the other behind. Perpendicular beams sometimes completed the frame. The image of the Saviour usually occupied the centre of the panel and the beams were decorated with sacred themes, the Last Supper for example, or even non-religious motifs (pl. 1). Sometimes the beams did not support a baldequin, but served as pedestals for sculpture or painted groups of wood carvings. Other types of religious works included large, wooden crosses, painted on both sides with motifs connected with the Virgin and St John, the sun and moon, and the symbols of the Evangelists.

Secular painting was as important in the life of the time as religious and ranged from decorations on saddles and wooden bowls to vast ceilings streaming with colour. Subjects from various sources are found side by side, drawn from Greek and Roman antiquities, medieval Europe and the rich resources of Muslim art. It should not be forgotten that Moorish painters worked side by side with Christian painters.

Although fully developed romanesque panel painting was produced through the 12th century and a good part of the 13th, some examples can be found in the 11th and some conventions survived into the 14th century. Most of the artists seem to have been laymen, living in towns like Barcelona, Perpignan, Vich, Gerona, Lérida or Seu de Urgell, which were important both as ecclesiastical and commercial centres. There were probably itinerant artists too and others living permanently in monasteries, but there is little information about their activities, unlike those of the manuscript illuminators. It is only in the last period that strong similarities are noticeable between some panel paintings and mural paintings. These are sometimes so close that they can be attributed to the same artist or workshop.

The oldest examples of Catalan painting are usually divided into two categories, corresponding to two separate groups of artists. In one, the work of painters such as those who did the altar frontals from Durro and Puigbó (pl. 2 and 3) has a narrative appeal, which gives it a strong, popular flavour, while the masters of the baldequin of Ribes (pl. 4) or the altar frontals from Esquius, Hix and Seu de Urgell (pl. 5) are obviously painters with a perfect mastery of geometric composition and the use of colour. The museums at Barcelona possess a particularly rich collection of the work of other great artists of the 12th century: the painters of altar frontals from Sant Martí Sescorts (pl. 6), El Coll (pl. 7), Dosmunts and the crosses from Cruïlles and Sant Joan les Fonts. The painter of the altar frontal from Sant Andreu at Capolat (pl. 8) is one of the most attractive of these artists through the skill and boldness of his simplifications. The panels of the Child-hood and Passion of Christ, which came originally from Sagas and are now in the Museo Arqueológico Diocesano at Solsona, are also attributed to him. The large panel from Tabérnoles, with nine bishops or mitred abbots, is exceptional in the skilfulness of its compo-sition and the elegance of the figures. In the second half of the 12th century, several altar frontals are painted in a popular manner, like those from Guils (Prado) and Llanars, which has been tentatively dated 1168. Among the artists of the late 12th century, the Master of Espinelves is considered one of the purest exponents of the classical romanesque tradition; his altar frontal can be seen at the museum at Vich (pl. 9). He also decorated an apse at Terrassa. Then about 1195, there were a number of artists, who painted in the Italian-Byzantine manner, which is clearly recognisable in the altar frontals from Valltarga (pl. 10) and Orellá for example. It is worth mentioning the connexion of both works with an altar frontal, signed by a certain *magister Alexander,* which is only known through some tracings and draw-ings. It disappeared in the last century from the church of St Genis des Fontaines in Roussil-lon, but M. de Bonnefoy saw it there about 1868.

There exist two dated works that show how over a considerable period this artistic style influenced painters with very different artistic backgrounds; one is by an artist who painted a miniature in 1195 for the monastery of Sant Martí del Canigó; the other is by an artist who put the date 1250 on an altar frontal, dedicated to St Martin and now in the Walters Art Gallery, Baltimore.

Although a number of painters were influenced by the style of the Master of Valltarga, it was the Masters of Aviá and Llussanés who blended it with native traditions. The representative work of the first is the altar frontal from Santa María at Aviá, which is so similar in style to that from Orellá that they may be two phases in the career of a single artist. He may also have painted an altar frontal dedicated to St Saturninus, originally from Rotgés, and another that came from the village of Rivesaltes in Roussillon. This like the former is dominated by the figure of the Saviour in majesty, but the four lateral scenes are dedicated to St Peter and St Paul. The altar frontal from Aviá, in an excellent state of preservation, is particularly remarkable for its marvellously rich colours and the variety of tone used for the modelling and shadows. The scene of the Nativity is probably more frequently reproduced than any other romanesque Catalan painting. The Master of Llussanés on the other hand was less influenced by Byzantine style and in modelling figures he often used white, either pure, or mixed with the predominant colour: bright blue, purple, red and yellow. His masterpieces are the paintings from Santa María at Llussá, which consist of an altar frontal with lateral panels (pl. 11) and a cross. It is one of the finest groups of paintings in the Museo Episcopal at Vich. His style is also recognisable in an altar frontal dedicated to St Michael (Barcelona, Museo de Arte de Cataluña) and

in the mural paintings (Solsona, Museo Arqueológico Diocesano) from the monastery dedicated
to St Paul of Narbona, near the village of
Casserres, which should not be confused with
the monastery of Sant Pere de Casserres, far
from any inhabited place, where the remains of
mural paintings in a much more archaic style
exist in the church.

The influence of these painters is reflected
in the work of a large number of minor artists;
it was popular in style, but often showed an
unusual talent and individuality. The best of
them is the painter of the baldequin from La
Llagona in which the monumental figure of the
Saviour is in strong contrast to the symbols of
the Evangelists, which are treated in a free and
highly expressive style. There were other
painters besides him, who were less talented,
but are interesting nevertheless; the Master of
Vidrá, for example, who painted an altar frontal
dedicated to St Hilary for the village of Vidrá
and also the panels of the Annunciation and
Visitation in the famous altarpiece of Engostrina
in French Cerdagne; from the same place, the
retable, now in the Instituto Amatller, Barcelona,
is a continuous panel surmounted by three
semi-circular arches, which depicts, in a
thoroughly popular style, Christ standing in the
centre and flanked by the Apostles; and the altar
frontal from Mosoll (pl. 12), which can be dated
about 1200, like the previous ones, which
possesses an unusual and attractive individuality.

The town of Gerona was one of the principal
artistic centres, but its great activity during the

gothic period probably accounts for the almost complete disappearance of earlier panel painting. The rare surviving examples are of high quality and remarkably varied. Although some works retain their geometrical severity even in the middle of the 12th century, like the cross from the Benedictine monastery of Sant Miquel at Cruïlles, there are others, like the cross beam from the apse of the same church (pl. 13), which are treated with a freedom anticipating the drawings and engravings on similar subjects in the following centuries.

There were two late groups of paintings in the extreme west of the region, which are particularly interesting. One comes from the region round Seu de Urgell and is remarkable for its brilliant colours, reds, greens and yellows, and the Byzantine influence on its style, probably derived from the mural paintings of Andorra. The work with the greatest similarity to these is the altar frontal from Ferrera, where the Apostles are divided into two groups under green arches, on either side of Christ in majesty. It is a completely classical composition going back to the age of the Emperor Constantine. From the little church of Vilar, near Encamp, Andorra, there has survived the only intact example of a painted altar, completely covered with figures. Almost cubic in form because of the smallness of the church, it consists of an altar frontal with Christ in the centre surrounded by four groups of Apostles; the border decorations and halos are in stucco relief. The lateral panels are quite independent of each other: one depicts three apostles in line, complementing the eight of the central panel; the other depicts the Assumption of the Virgin. The second artistic centre was either situated at Lérida or Roda, the ancient episcopal seat. A large number of works, recognisable from their backgrounds of gilt stucco in relief, came from this region. The oldest works are probably the altar frontals from Tresserra and Betesa (pl. 14), one dedicated to St Andrew, the other to the Virgin. The colour range is muted, with a predominance of cherry red, olive green and grey-blue. The altar frontal from Chía, dedicated to saint Martin, has an unusual interest because it is signed by a certain *Johannes Pintor*. Then there are a few isolated works: a small reliquary from the Cathedral of Roda, a painted cross of unknown provenance (Barcelona, Museo de Arte de Cataluña) and an altar frontal, dedicated to the Virgin, from the church at Cardet, in the valley of Boí. This group ends with various, brilliantly painted, early works, all from the valley of Boí: an altar frontal dedicated to St Peter, dominated, like the one from Chía, by the seated figure of the titular saint; another dedicated to St Clement, with scenes arranged on two registers; and an apse beam, discovered at Cardet and covered with nonreligious motifs, pairs of birds and animals, fights between warriors and monsters, which may have been the pedestal for a group of sculptures. All these illustrate a local or diocesan continuity, in which local development is more important than external influences.

In the centre of the diocese of Urgell, a similar development can be seen in a number of very fine works, but here it led to an extremely linear stylisation, which already had a close affinity to gothic. The trajectory curves from the monumental baldequin from Tost and its direct reflection in the paintings from Oros and Os de Tremp, which represent St Peter and St Paul, to the baldequin from Tabérnoles in which the figure of Christ, surrounded by four angels with shaded, or rather draperies in muted colours is in contrast to the previous works, although the composition still follows the same canon.

Further to the east, but still partly within the episcopal territory, the transition from romanesque to gothic continued in the work of the Master of Soriguerola. Although his manner is essentially romanesque, he is a gothic artist also, at least in the way he modelled his draperies. However, when he borrows certain, typically gothic, architectural elements, as in the altar frontal of St Christopher, one of his early works, their effect is just as artificial as the Mudejar strap-work, which he also used. His genuinely romanesque character is confirmed, moreover, by the existence of a disciple, or epigon, with a very archaic manner, called the Master of Greixa.

As most of the Barcelona churches were redecorated or built in the middle of the 13th century, the panel paintings in them are generally late romanesque. The expansionist drive that reached its peak with the conquest of Majorca in 1229 and Valencia nine years later, explains the existence of panel paintings in an identical style at Barcelona and Palma. The altar frontal from Santa Perpetua at Moguda

(Barcelona, Museo Diocesano) is an excellent example of this art, which preserves the romanesque traditions, in spite of the gothic frames. The retable of St Bernard, originally in the House of the Templars at Palma, and some fragments from paintings of the legend of St Ursula, discovered at Artá and now, like the St Bernard retable, at Palma, all belong to the same group although their draughtsmanship is superior and their colouring richer. The style of these works has affinities with the numerous, non-religious mural paintings in Barcelona and those in the monastery of Sant Cugat del Vallés.

Finally, before ending this rapid survey, a wood ceiling in one of the rooms of the Palacio Aguilar at Barcelona must be mentioned. It illustrates episodes from the conquest of Majorca, and is richly painted in a style where the mixture of gothic and Moorish elements with traditional romanesque is very characteristic of Barcelona painting of the period.

PLATES

1. BEAM FROM VINYOLES DE PORTABELLA. PRINCIPAL SUBJECT WITH A HUMAN HEAD. *Museo Episcopal, Vich.*

2. MARTYRDOM OF ST QUIRICUS. ALTAR FRONTAL FROM DURRO. *Museo de Arte de Cataluña, Barcelona.*

3. ST MARTIN DIVIDING HIS CLOAK WITH A BEGGAR. ALTAR FRONTAL FROM PUIGBÓ. *Museo Episcopal, Vich.*

4. CHRIST IN MAJESTY WITH ANGELS. BALDEQUIN FROM RIBES. *Museo Episcopal, Vich.*

5. ALTAR FRONTAL FROM SEU DE URGELL. ENSEMBLE. *Museo de Arte de Cataluña, Barcelona.*

6. SCENE FROM THE MARTYRDOM OF ST MARGARET. ALTAR FRONTAL FROM SANT MARTÍ SESCORTS. *Museo Episcopal, Vich.*

7. VIRGIN AND CHILD WITH SYMBOLS OF THE EVANGELISTS. ALTAR FRONTAL FROM EL COLL. *Museo Episcopal, Vich.*

8. DETAIL FROM AN EPISODE IN THE LIFE OF ST ANDREW. ALTAR FRONTAL FROM CAPOLAT. *Museo Episcopal, Vich.*

9. CHRIST'S ENTRY INTO JERUSALEM. ALTAR FRONTAL FROM ESPINELVES. *Museo Episcopal, Vich.*

10. ST JOHN THE EVANGELIST WITH THE VIRGIN. ALTAR FRONTAL FROM VALLTARGA. *Museo de Arte de Cataluña, Barcelona.*

11. ST JOHN THE EVANGELIST WITH THE VIRGIN SURROUNDED BY THE SEVEN GIFTS OF THE HOLY SPIRIT. SIDE PANEL FROM THE ALTAR FROM LLUSSÁ. *Museo Episcopal, Vich.*

12. KING BALTHAZAR ON HORSEBACK. DETAIL OF THE ALTAR FROM MOSOLL. *Museo de Arte de Cataluña, Barcelona.*

13. ECCLESIASTICAL PROCESSION. BEAM FROM SANT MIQUEL AT CRUÏLLES. DETAIL. *Museo Diocesano, Gerona.*

14. THE ANNUNCIATION. ALTAR FRONTAL FROM BETESA. *Museo de Arte de Cataluña, Barcelona.*

15. PANELS FROM A CEILING AT THE PALACIO AGUILAR, BARCELONA. *Museo de Arte de Cataluña, Barcelona.*

I

DNOP A E NRIS

3

4

5

MARGA
RITA

MARGAI
TA

GARITA · VELIŞ

6

8

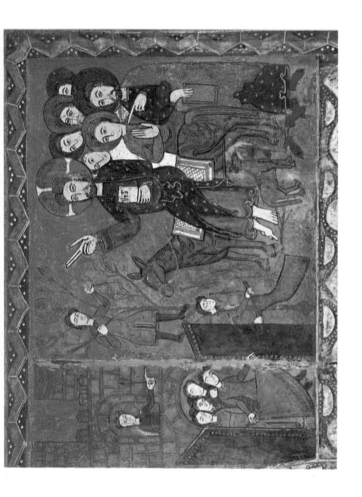

9

BALTASAR

MARIA

12

13